Productivity Hacks for Recruiters

How to Manage your Recruiting Time Well

By: Jonathan Kidder

Table of Contents

Chapter 1: Setting up for Success — 7

Chapter 2: Staying Organized — 13

Chapter 3: Time Management Best Practices — 23

Chapter 4: How to Manage your Calendar — 31

Chapter 5: Creating Good Habits — 50

Chapter 6: Tracking your time — 57

Chapter 7: Creating Goals and Tracking KPI Sourcing Metrics — 65

Chapter 8: Productivity Tools — 70

Chapter 9: Automation Tools — 86

Chapter 10: Working with Hiring Managers — 100

Summary — 107

Conclusion — 111

Appendix — 112

This book was written to help recruiting professionals become more productive and manage their time well.

<u>What makes a recruiter successful?</u>

Is it someone who works long hours with a jam-packed schedule?

The short answer is: a recruiter who is productive and well organized throughout the full-cycle recruiting process might not be someone who is working at their maximum level.

Outside of being productive and well-organized a recruiter must have intelligence, a sense of optimism, and be able to problem solve while being solution oriented. There are many ways to remain productive and organized without over exerting yourself professionally.

In my decade-long career, I have witnessed how successful recruiters manage themselves versus others who have gotten too overwhelmed by their recruiting duties. The successful ones have mastered their schedule and have created effective recruiting routines and positive habits which in turn have caused them to make more hires and have a life outside of their job.

Yes, I'm here to say that you can indeed have a life outside of the recruiting field! A majority of recruiters unfortunately have on the job training and may well learn how to do things the wrong way depending on where they have worked. Agency based recruiters are taught that speed and long hours are the ways to succeed long term. I started my career at a staffing agency. We would have daily meetings on team updates. The managers praised recruiters that would skip lunch and even work after hours to get projects and reqs filled. This created a poor mindset and environment. Many recruiters have experienced environments like the one that I had. In this book, I will help teach you how to manage your time well, becoming more productive, organized, and not having to overwork yourself to extreme levels.

When I hear recruiters say that they must work outside of work hours or work weekends I don't think that is a positive thing or some badge of honor. They sometimes pride themselves on the fact that they are working above and beyond what is expected. But, at the end of the day a HIRE offer-accept is the most important part. You could be working less than 40 hours a week and making the most hires on your team, versus someone pushing 60 hours and not delivering anything. The recruiter making more hires will be the one getting recognized and ultimately promoted long term.

The book will show you how to master your time and schedule, remain organized, and be productive all while working less hours within your work week. There are many tools and tricks to automate mundane tasks. My goal is to help the overstressed and overworked recruiters. I'll accomplish this by showcasing routine tips and tricks using tools and other hacks to work smarter and not harder.

Who should read this book:
- Sourcers, Recruiters, and Recruiting Managers looking to become more efficient.
- Recruiting professionals looking to conquer a work week within a 9 to 5 time frame.
- Individuals looking to excel and become more productive and organized.

In the Productivity Hacks book, you'll learn how to:

- Learn how to set yourself up for long term success
- Learn how to stay organized and productive
- Time management best practices
- Mastering daily calendar and other recruiting routines
- Creating good habits
- Managing your calendar and schedule
- Tracking your time
- Creating daily, weekly, and monthly goals
- Creating a sourcing tracking KPI document
- Automation tools to make you more productive
- Email Mail merging tips
- Automating reach outs and follow ups

Chapter 1: Setting up for Success

Recruiting is not a sprint it's a marathon!

A hack is an informal term that describes a strategy or technique for managing one's time or activities more efficiently. A recruiter's time will either make or break you at your company. I would sometimes say to myself - if I had more time in the day I could accomplish X, Y, Z. I never had enough time to accomplish everything all within one given day or even in a week.

I'm not describing hacking into a computer system but rather finding ways to cut down on mundane recruiting tasks within your day. On top of that, there are many hidden distractors or time killers that you might be doing without fully realizing it. Scrolling your phone, searching Facebook, or ESPN can suck up valuable time. You may sit onsite next to a cube of recruiters and might not even realize the drain on productivity. Most recruiters are extroverted. At one job, I had a recruiter who seemed compelled to just talk 2-3 hours a day about unrelated topics. I realized this right away and decided to time block rooms across the office and not to distract myself from much needed sourcing duties.

Most of the time, I would see other seasoned recruiters on my team accomplish so much within a day and I became curious on how they worked through so many obstacles within a time frame. Throughout my career I would always ask this simple question - how do you do what you do here?

I received simple responses to my questions:

1. Create a daily list of things that you want to accomplish. Including goals that your recruiting manager can hold you accountable for.
2. Time block your calendar for sourcing or other needed activities.
3. Block your calendar for a lunch break - it's good to take a mental break.
4. Commit to things that you know that you can accomplish.
5. Setting clear and realistic expectations with hiring managers and interviewing teams.

6. Use your PTO time well - learn when your company is in a slow period (often November or December) and take the time off.
7. Invest in using tools to automate mundane tasks to improve productivity.

Everything listed will help you stay refreshed and productive throughout your career.

In this book, I will break down various categories and highlight simple yet effective hacks that will help you improve on time and efficiency. The chapters will ultimately help you learn to become more efficient and more organized in your recruiting day.

Saying "No" well
An important area where recruiters sometimes have a hard time dealing with is saying "no" to time wasting tasks. I was inspired by a fellow recruiter Brian Fink on this topic; he's spoken about this on several occasions.

When people ask you — even in a perfectly respectful way — to attend a meeting, perform a task, take their phone call, or participate in a project, remember there is freedom in telling that person "NO". Even if they are serious opportunities, even if it will only take 15 minutes, even if it's something that everyone else does, I'd like to avoid it.

Having a meeting is like throwing a distraction on your calendar. It doesn't merely cause you to switch from one task to another; it changes the mode in which you work. Remember, there is no shame in saying it.

People will respect you for being honest and move on. If they continue to pressure you into saying "yes", then politely explain to them that you feel like you wouldn't be able to spend the proper amount of time that this project would require. This will make you a more dependable person because you can allocate more time to the tasks that you are already doing.

Go with your gut
Sometimes a candidate might not be the best fit for your role. You will need to assess the value of your time. If a candidate doesn't meet your hiring bar, then don't proceed with a phone screen. It's that simple – a lot of junior level recruiters will talk with anyone. But as you gain experience you will understand that your time is important.

Your health depends on it
"As we age, it is important to de-stress our lives and direct more of our attention to things that we truly enjoy doing. The time in our lives that we worked 12-hour days has passed and is no longer required. It is all right to do this in your 20's and 30's but once you reach 45, it is time to eliminate the clutter in your lives and evaluate what is most important." - Brian Fink

You should have a good reason every time you say "yes"
Assess whether the task is doable. Will the task add value to my life? If I do it, what task will I not be getting done? Set boundaries in your mind for what you can accomplish without feeling resentful and stick to them. Do what is important to you, your family, or your job and so "no" to the rest.

Communication is everything
At times, being in constant contact with each candidate can be daunting as you alternate between multiple recruiting assignments. And many candidates fall into the same frame. However, to be successful in recruiting, we must keep in touch with each of our candidates. Choose the channel that works best for you. In our view, email is the sure-shot

channel followed by a phone call. You can automate follow ups and have pre-vetted templates to send out using your ATS or other email tools.

Ultimately, you will need to over-communicate but you can do this by using automated tools.

Chapter 2: Staying Organized

VUCA stands for volatility, uncertainty, complexity, and ambiguity. It describes the situation of constant, unpredictable change that is now the norm in certain industries. Recruiters live and breathe VUCA every single day. Thankfully, there are ways to thrive in this constant uncertainty.

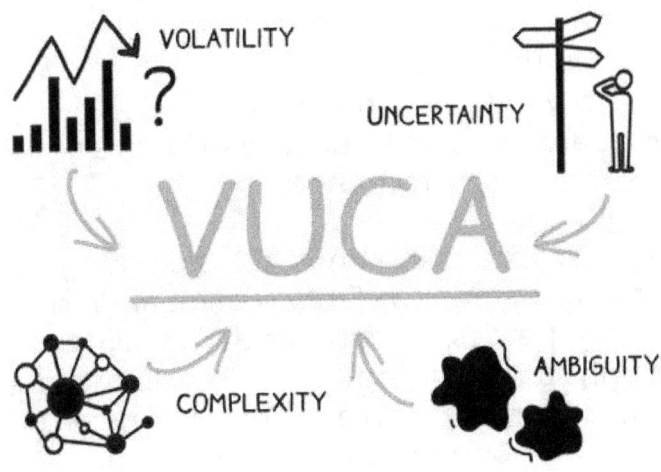

(Source: https://www.streetsweb.co.uk)

Volatile: Change is rapid and unpredictable in its nature and extent.

Uncertainty: The present is unclear and the future is uncertain.

Complex: Many different, interconnected factors come into play, with the potential to cause chaos and confusion.

Ambiguous: There is a lack of clarity or awareness about situations.

A VUCA environment can:

- Destabilize people and make them anxious.
- Sap their motivation.
- Thwart their career moves.
- Cause people to be unproductive and remain unorganized.

The key to improving on VUCA is creating a clear vision, creating clarity with goals and tracking metrics, creating understanding through standardizing your full cycle process, and finally creating an agile environment to make continuous improvement to your process. The remainder of this book will cover ways to make improvements and make you a more productive recruiter.

Getting Organized

If there's one thing that can make or break your work week, it's organization. With proper organization, you'll be able to get more done in less time, allowing you to do your best on every recruitment need that comes your way. If you leave your process unstructured, however, you could find yourself getting sidetracked by unnecessary tasks and losing focus on what really matters. Don't worry; there's a simple fix. By planning, you can prevent distractions from hijacking your recruiting efforts entirely.

Organize your computer's desktop

First and foremost, you should do a thorough clean-up of your computer's desktop. Organize it by creating folders that represent each client/project/type of file/type of document.

For example, if you have more than one client, create separate folders for each one on your computer's desktop (e.g., Hiring Manager A and Hiring Manager B). If you also have several projects for each HM, create subfolders (Project A, Project B...) within those folders.

This will help in two ways: First, it will make it easier to find files you rely on to complete your recruitment tasks, streamlining your overall process; Second, it maintains your professionalism, as you'll be far less likely to accidentally mix up client documents and prove you're focused on their needs.

Create a To-Do list

A to-do list is an essential tool for planning your week at work—regardless of your industry. You should create one for every week ahead of time so that when Monday arrives, you have a clear understanding of what needs to be accomplished on each day. Make sure that each task has its due date and time written down somewhere so you can keep track of their progress throughout the week.

Organize your schedule using a calendar or app like Google Calendar or Todoist. These tools allow you to create events in advance; this way they won't slip through the cracks due to forgetfulness! They also allow you schedule other people's activities as well as meetings with clients, if necessary, which can be incredibly helpful for the modern recruiter.

To take things a step further, try separating your list into different categories:

- **Priority:** Is the task of high importance? Or is it one that can be pushed to the side for a bit?
- **Time:** Some tasks might need immediate attention—be sure to note these.

- **Hiring Managers:** If you're working with multiple HMs, consider including this information for extra clarity.
- **Topic and type:** Not every task will be the same. Help yourself out by noting whether you'll need to put your networking hat on, prepare to meet with a candidate, or something else.

In practice, do something small and measure the impact! Rinse and repeat.

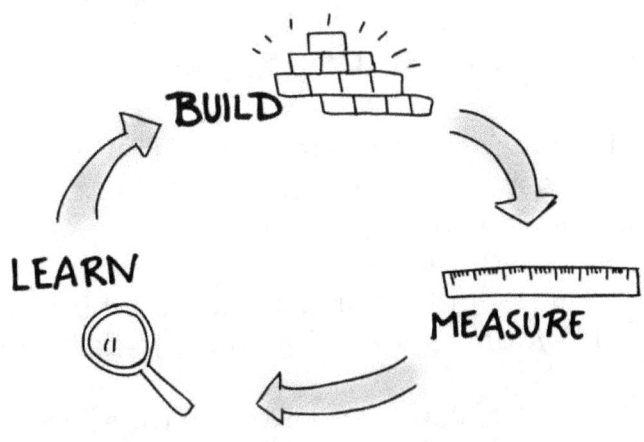

Does it work?
Yes, do again.
No, iterate.

Hypothesis, test assumption, & repeat.

Create deadlines for your to-do items

When planning your week, it's just as important to include a deadline for each task. It's so easy to say, "I will do this later" and never get around to it. Still, your deadlines should be realistic so that you can still accomplish them in the time frame specified. If you miss the deadline, make sure that you add more time into your schedule to grant yourself some mobility to catch up.

Plan for distractions

The life of a 21st century recruiter is full of these. Though they're not entirely avoidable, you *can* prepare for them in advance.

Try to plan for potential distractions when outlining your week to avoid getting derailed.

For instance, if you suspect that a meeting will run long and leave no time for lunch, try pushing back some of your following responsibilities to make up for it. Though your work is important, don't be afraid to put yourself first.

Understanding Parteo's Principle and Parkson's Law

Parteo's Principle

The Pareto principle states that for many outcomes, roughly 80% of consequences come from 20% of causes. Not all tasks are of equal value so take some time to understand the value of your effort. It highlights the importance of taking a strategic approach to prioritization and delegation in order to optimize efficiency and time management.

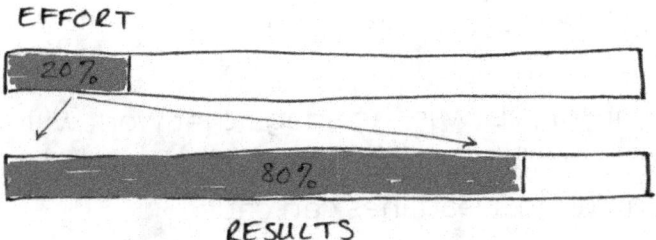

(Source: https://metaphoricmath.com)

The Pareto Principle is counterintuitive; to assume cause equals effect is a 50/50 fallacy. Our tendency toward linear thinking is often an oversimplification of reality, where cause and effect rarely demonstrate equality.

The indirect correlation between input and output reveals that all inputs are not created equal. The Pareto ratio is variable; it could be 70/30, 90/10, or 99/1 – in fact, the two numbers do not even have to add up to 100 because they reflect completely separate measures. (Source: metaphoricmath.com)

Apply this idea into your recruiting process:

What are the 20% elements where you can focus your efforts in order to achieve 80% of the results?

Parkinson's Law

Parkinson's Law is the adage that work will expand to fill the time allotted for its completion. Deadlines can cause procrastination or even prompt people to fill their time with trivial matters. Do not fill your time with un-need mundane tasks.

When implementing Parkinson's Law, look for those little time-fillers, like email and social media reading, that you might usually think take ten, twenty, or event thirty minutes.

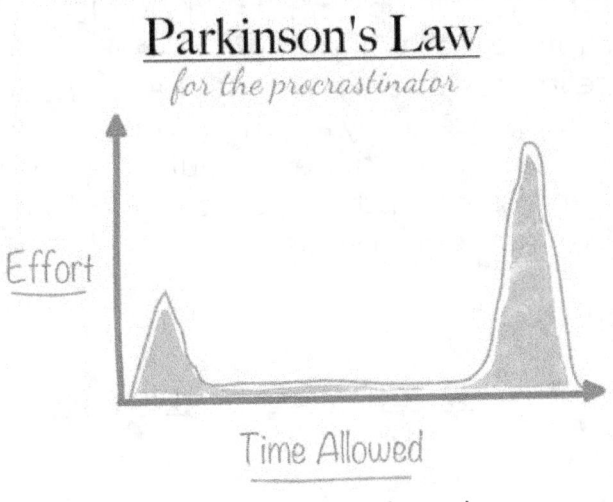

(Source: Lifehack.org)

Keep the future in sight, but don't forget to reflect

When you're planning for the end of a week, it's important to keep in mind that sometimes schedules change. You might need to move things around or shift priorities when something unexpected comes up. But it's always worth taking some time at the end of each workweek to plan out your tasks for the next one, even if those tasks are just tentative ideas at this point.

Set Goals to Avoid Time Waste

The end of a workweek is also a great time to reflect on what you have accomplished over the past seven days and review what went well with your recruiting efforts and why. It can also be helpful to see where there are still areas where improvement could be made. Though there isn't necessarily anything wrong with not getting everything done on your list every week (or even every month), it's always good practice to learn from our mistakes.

Review your weekly goals list:

Wins
- X
- Y
- X

Challenges
- X. path to green:
- Y. path to green:
- X. path to green:

Metrics
- X (% change week on week)
- Y (how does it fit into the bigger picture)
- Z (green/orange/red status)

Chapter 3: Time Management Best Practices

Whether you're a seasoned recruiter or just starting out, it's important to have the right time management practices in place. This is especially true if you work for yourself and need to manage your own schedule. Here are some of my favorite best practices I've learned over the years that will help you make the most of each day:

6 strategies for recruiters

To take your recruiting skills to the next level, you need to understand the best time management methodologies within our business.

1. Agile

The Agile methodology is a way to manage a project by breaking it up into several phases. It involves constant collaboration with stakeholders and continuous improvement at every stage. Once the work begins, teams' cycle through a process of planning, executing, and evaluating. Great milestones and goals for area.

- How can we adapt to changing situations?
- How can we set weekly/monthly goals?
- How can we discover and understand our customer's needs?

Three simple truths of recruiting an Agile environment:

1. It's impossible to know everything at the beginning of a project
2. Whatever you do know is guaranteed to change
3. There will always be more to do than time and money will allow

2. Kanban

This simple system relies on recruiters sorting their tasks into three categories: "To Do," "Doing," and "Done." When placed into columns on a physical or digital whiteboard, these "stages" of tasks can help you refrain from taking on too many tasks at once and—most importantly—feel the satisfaction of marking something as complete.

- How can we improve how we get things done?
- How can we focus on finishing work?
- How can we force ruthless prioritization?

3. Inbox-Zero

This tool labels and prioritizes your inbox, ensuring you receive only receive notifications when you want them and allowing you to delegate e-mails to someone else.

4. Eat the frog technique

Inspired by Mark Twain's saying, "Eat a live frog first thing in the morning and nothing worse will happen to you the rest of the day," this strategy relies on completing your most complex tasks right away. Doing so will help you kickstart momentum and focus on other tasks without stress.

5. The Eisenhower technique

You'll organize and prioritize your tasks into four categories with this method (it's helpful to draw a box for this):

1. **Do:** Urgent *and* important.
2. **Delegate:** Urgent but not important.
3. **Schedule:** Important but not urgent.
4. **Delete:** Not urgent *and* not important.

6. The Timeboxing technique

Finally, this method encourages recruiters to set specific periods of time in which they can only focus on one activity. For instance, one 30-

minute "timebox" may be reserved for sourcing candidates, whereas the next interval is reserved for checking your email.

Allow yourself a specific amount of time to complete something in advanced. When the time is finished, step away from it. I time-box my calendar to focus solely on sourcing activities. You can use this to stay focused, energized, and measures progress quickly.

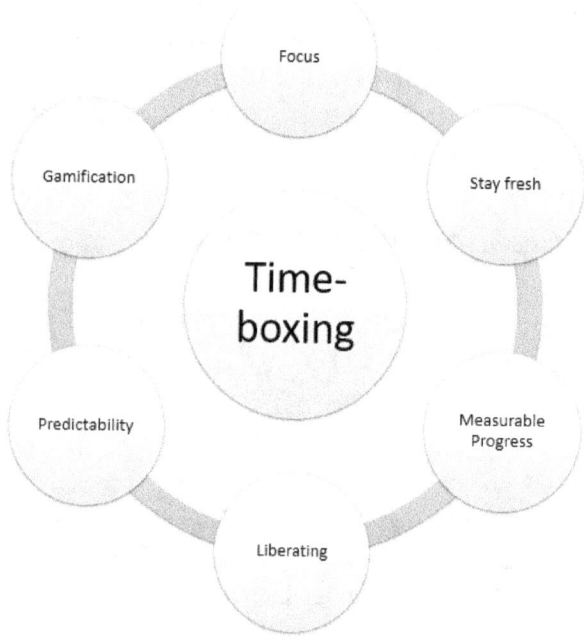

Avoid the multi-tasking myth

Every recruiter will have days where they will need to do several things within a quick turnaround. They might think conquering all these tasks at once is a good thing. In reality, it could be a horrible mistake.

"Multi-tasking does not exist, instead its constant context switching which is detrimental to quality and speed of work. Instead, focus on doing less, but better." – Unknown

The best option is to create structure. A more seasoned recruiter will know how to push back various duties to set realistic and attainable outcomes. If you don't learn how to manage your day, you will most likely get drained and burnt out from such overzealous requirements.

Unfortunately, many recruiters put high expectations on themselves—I'm guilty of doing that myself. But coaching from my recruiting manager has helped me to create manageable tasks and goals, and I know that doing the same will only help your career flourish in the long run.

Use templates for your emails and other communications

You're already familiar with the importance of templates when it comes to writing cover letters and other documents. For a recruiter, they remain just as helpful of a tool.

Templates can be incredibly useful in any situation where you find yourself needing to churn the same content repeatedly, such as when drafting standard emails or creating a job description. Obviously, using them during your daily tasks will allow you to save time, which is a precious commodity for recruiters who are perpetually juggling multiple projects at once.

So, if you have certain types of tasks that come up often (e.g., sending out interview reminders), try streamlining them with a template. Be careful not to make yours overly specific, as you'll need to adjust a few sections according to its recipient and/or subject matter.

Ask for feedback from candidates

No matter how much experience you have in recruiting, it's always a good idea to ask for feedback from candidates after they complete your recruitment process. This can be done through email or phone call, but the most important thing is that you receive an honest opinion regarding the overall experience.

You should ask what they liked about the process, what could be improved upon, where they felt confused and more to receive an objective second opinion regarding your workflow. This will not only help you improve your success rate moving forward, but it will also reveal any gaps in your time-management strategy that need fixing.

Collaborate

Collaborate with your colleagues, share best practices and feedback with them. This will help you to work more efficiently as a team. If possible, delegate tasks to other team members, such as scheduling interviews, to lighten your load.

Don't over-promise

When you're working with a client, it's important to be realistic about what you can deliver. If you know that you don't have the time for a specific project, don't sign on anyways only to deliver something less than expected. As a rule of thumb, be careful not to set expectations too high if there's no way to meet them—or if you *suspect* there's no way to. This is especially important when working with new clients or those who may not know as much about the field you do, as they may be mistakenly asking for too much without knowing it's out of reach for most recruiters.

Dedicate time for yourself

By nature, a recruiter's job needs them to be more productive than the average person at work—exceptional communication and time management skills are a must. It's easy to get overwhelmed by these priorities, yet learning these abilities is not impossible. Remember:

Productivity is not just about getting work done but also enjoying what you do. So, if you're feeling stressed by all the tasks on your plate, don't forget to take some breaks—even just five minutes away from the computer can make a huge difference!

Taking regular breaks can help you to stay fresh and focused throughout the day. Use the Pomodoro Technique, working in short, focused bursts of 25 minutes, with 5-minute breaks in between.

Pro tip: Turn off your slack messages and allocate time at the end of your day to respond to team chats.

Chapter 4: How to Manage Email and Calendar Scheduling

Managing emails and scheduling is a tricky thing for recruiters, as so much of our duties rely on constant communication with others. However, there are plenty of hacks you can use to make sure you stay on top of your most pressing priorities all week long. Here are some tips for managing your email and calendar scheduling.

How to properly organize your email and calendar

Without a proper system in place, it could only take one day for your process to be overcome by these two essential resources. Though both rely on different tools, you'll find that having efficient email and calendar organization will help take your efforts to the next level. Some general considerations you'll want to keep in mind include:

1. Choosing the right platform

Not every solution is built the same. Take time to review different platforms to see which one best suit your needs. For instance, Calendly's automated meeting scheduler could prove vital for a recruiter focused on candidate interviews, whereas Gmail's integrations are a must-have for one who works heavily within the Google ecosystem.

Example: *LinkedIn's Scheduler allows you to schedule meetings directly within the platform.*

Schedule candidate - Quick Settings

Settings for this candidate. To change default settings, go to preferences. Refresh the page to apply changes.

Meeting duration	Link expiration date
30 minutes ▼	1 week ▼

Cancel | **Save changes**

2. Scheduling your scheduling time

Yes, even your planning needs its own planning. Set aside an hour or two at the start of each week to sit down and plot out the details of your schedule.

3. Utilizing reminders

Emails and calendars aren't the only platforms that rely on reminders, but they might matter most in these instances. A digital nudge could be the difference between completing an important priority on-time and accidentally letting it slip by.

4. Creating an email signature

Email signatures are a great way to add a personal touch to your messages. You can include things like your name, phone number, company website, and even social media accounts if you want. On a practical note, this could save you from having to send out additional emails detailing this very information: By having it already included in your signature, your recipients won't have to continue the conversation any longer than necessary.

Pro Tip: Include your upcoming PTO in your email signature. It lets everyone know in advance that you'll be out and gives you something to look forward to every time you see it.

Email management tips

Emails are often where recruiters need the most help staying organized. There are a few proven strategies you can begin gradually adopting into your workflow to make the process easier.

1. Use labels, categories, and folders

These features are found in virtually every platform and can quickly help turn your email from a cluttered mess into a neat, streamlined communication tool. Since they're customizable by nature, don't worry if they look different than your colleagues'—if they're optimized for your brain and workflow, you're set for success.

2. Don't set responses aside

It's tempting to pretend like you didn't see an email. But, if you're able to respond to a message after reading it, it's always best to do so immediately. Try following the 1-minute rule: If it takes less than 1-minute to write a reply, don't file it away for later.

3. Only Handle it Once (OHIO)

This method will help prevent you from mulling over an email over and over. As soon as you begin interacting with an email (whether you're writing or reading it), don't move on until the task is complete.

4. Strategize your cold outreach

Learn how to use mail merge effectively. Use tools to measure clicks and responses on each of your email campaigns. Use tools like Gem or

Lemlist to create email sequences campaigns. Remember that on average it does take roughly 4-6 emails before you hear back from a lead.

5. Create Email Templates

Whether you're sending a cold recruiting email, interview request, a job offer, a rejection email or even a crisis communication email to your internal team— it helps to have sample email templates ready for each scenario.

That way you don't have to recreate an email from scratch and waste time in the process. Following templates also standardizes the process and ensures a consistent experience. Remember: templates are just the starting point. You must also look at customizing them according to each candidate's profile and requirements before hitting send. Make sure you sound professional and natural.

You can also set up auto-replies and send timely responses to engage and acknowledge candidates. This gets easier when you use an ATS that has auto reply, which lets you automatically respond to each application with a customized message.

6. Pause your inbox

Another easy way to mitigate your email time without going cold turkey would be to pause your inbox using some clever Gmail coding or an app like Inbox Pause. This prevents emails from clogging your inbox for a set period, so you're not distracted by incoming messages as you're working on more important tasks.

Gmail hacks

As one of the largest email services in the globe, Google has created quite a few "hacks" professionals can use to keep their efforts as organized and productive as possible. Here are a few you'll find useful throughout your recruiting journey.

- **Enable keyboard shortcuts:** These will save you time and can be a big help when you're trying to send an email in a hurry. Read up on Gmail's available shortcuts and keep them on a piece of paper nearby to get into the practice of using them.
- **Use canned responses for repetitive tasks:** As a recruiter, you'll receive many similar inquiries that can be responded to with the same message repeatedly. Gmail allows you to create canned responses (or "templates") that can be pasted in just a few clicks.
- **Use the Star feature:** You'll inevitably have some conversations and contacts

that are more important than others. By "starring" these emails, you'll be able to section them off for easier access.
- **Try out drag and drop:** This neat trick allows you to drag attachments into any email, saving you from having to deal with a few extra clicks. You can even drag and drop emails into your computer's desktop to save it as a file.

Outlook hacks

Another popular service for several industries, you might find yourself opting for Outlook's email solution (or both!). Again, there are a few special tips you can keep in your toolbox for a more productive communication process.

Outlook Rules:

When activated, Outlook can automatically file your emails for you through the "Rules" feature. Doing so can help you organize emails by sender and/or subject. Use rules to automatically sort incoming emails into specific folders based on criteria such as sender, subject, or keywords. This can save time and keep your inbox organized.

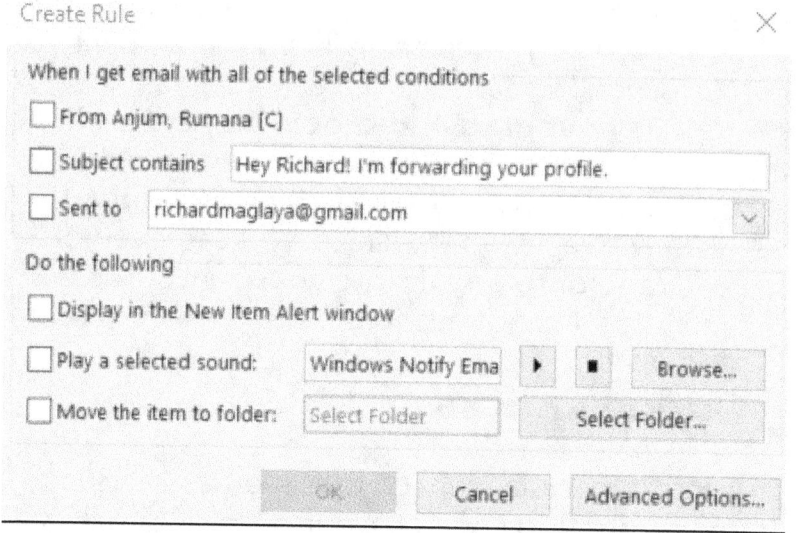

Use templates:

Create email templates for messages that you frequently send. This can save time and ensure consistency in your communication.

Create Categories

Don't overlook the importance of visuals when it comes to your organizational needs. Outlooks categories can also be separated by several colored tags, keeping you from sorting through individual emails to find the right contact or reply.

Schedule emails:

Use the "Delay Delivery" feature to schedule emails to be sent at a later time. This can help you avoid sending emails during non-business hours and keep your inbox from becoming overwhelming.

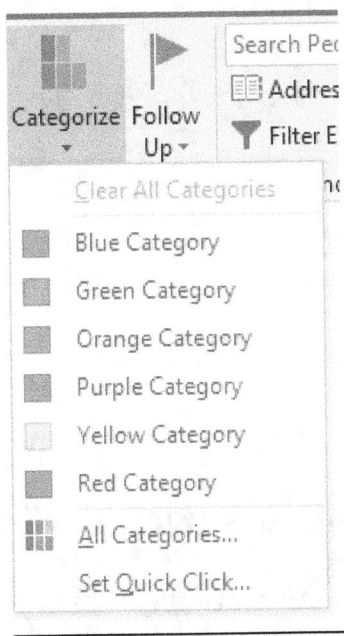

Create follow-ups

You can also use categories to "flag" which emails need attention. This may be particularly useful for conversations that span more than a few days and require reminders.

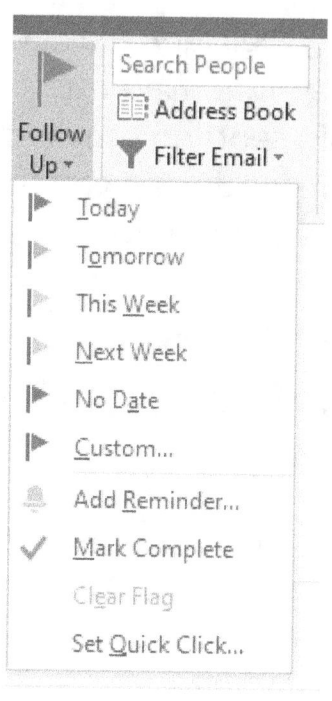

Filter your Inbox Automatically

Outlook also automatically filters your emails according to a few general categories for quick access.

Outlook filters allow you to organize your emails based on certain criteria. Here are some examples of Outlook filters:

Unread emails: This filter allows you to see only the emails that you haven't read yet. To use this filter, click on the "Filter Email" button and select "Unread."

Flagged emails: This filter shows all emails that you have flagged for follow-up. To use this filter, click on the "Filter Email" button and select "Flagged."

Emails with attachments: This filter allows you to see only the emails that have attachments. To use this filter, click on the "Filter Email" button and select "Has Attachments."

Emails from a specific sender: This filter allows you to see only the emails from a specific sender. To use this filter, click on the "Filter Email" button and select "From."

Emails with a specific subject line: This filter allows you to see only the emails with a specific subject line. To use this filter, click on the "Filter Email" button and select "Subject."

Emails within a specific date range: This filter allows you to see only the emails that were sent or received within a specific date range. To use this filter, click on the "Filter Email" button and select "Date."

Emails that are categorized: This filter allows you to see only the emails that are categorized. To use this filter, click on the "Filter Email" button and select "Categorized."

Emails that are marked as important: This filter allows you to see only the emails that are marked as important. To use this filter, click on the "Filter Email" button and select "Important.

Filter example:

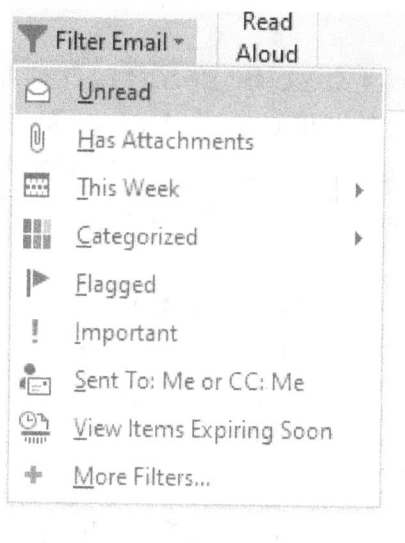

Have Outlook Read out loud the names - for correct pronunciation

Call people by their name and make a genuine effort of pronouncing it correctly. You would be surprised how delighted people feel when someone calls/spells out their name correctly, especially if it is difficult to pronounce or write. If the first name is not shortened, ask them politely if you can call them by the shortened form.

Export Outlook contacts into a CSV tracker document

The process for exporting contacts into a CSV file may vary slightly depending on the device or platform you are using. However, the general steps are as follows:

- Open the application or program where your contacts are stored. This could be your phone's contacts app, email client, or online address book.

- Look for an option to export or backup your contacts. In most cases, this can be found under the settings or options menu.

- Choose the file format you want to export your contacts as. Select CSV (Comma Separated Values) as your file format.

- Depending on your platform, you may be prompted to choose which fields you want to include in the CSV file. Choose the fields that you want to include in your file and click "Export" or "Save."

- Choose a location on your device where you want to save the CSV file.

- Name the file and click "Save" or "Export."

- You can then import this CSV file into a sourcing tracker document.

How to go out of office (and not destroy your schedule)

Occasionally taking time away from your work life can be a great way to refuel and reinvigorate your efforts, but the prospect of dealing with your schedule before and after a vacation can make it hard to enjoy your break.

Fortunately, the digital platforms you already use for scheduling purposes have a few solutions to make the transition to as easy as possible.

1. Set your calendars

Even if you've already blocked off a section of time in advance, it's worth putting your calendar software into "out of office" mode. Google Calendar and Outlook will automatically decline all meetings scheduled within your specified timeframe.

Note: You can also put your LinkedIn out of office and direct visitors to others on your team for a point of contact.

2. Create an email autoreply

Being in the business of communication, you're likely to receive a few emails while you're away. It's good etiquette to provide a response explaining your absence—but thanks to technology, you don't have to write it out yourself.

Using your email service's auto-response feature, draft a brief message detailing information like:
- The dates you'll be out of office
- If applicable, the contact information of other people who may be able to help instead
- Whether you'll respond to the email upon your return, or if the sender should send a follow-up after your return date

3. Don't forget to turn off your settings once you're back

Schedule a reminder to turn off these settings once you've come back from your break. You'll want to avoid accidentally turning away potential candidates with a vacation auto-response—even though you're back in office!

General scheduling and communication tips for a better candidate experience

The work of a recruiter doesn't stop short at software hacks and tricks. There are always areas where you can improve your process and ensure your efforts don't go to waste! Here are some final considerations to keep in mind when communicating with candidates using your newly acquired email and scheduling skills.

1. Following up

Automating reminder and follow-up emails is one of the easiest recruiting automation hacks because it is likely a feature of a tool you already use, like your ATS or technical assessment platform. An email reminder before an upcoming interview is an easy way to increase the number of touchpoints that create a positive experience for a candidate.

These emails don't need to be especially personal; they just need to be helpful. This is totally possible with a templated, automated email.

Schedule follow ups with future leads. Say a lead wants you to follow up with them in 6-12 months, use your calendar and save a meeting for that follow up date.

Use your ATS system to automate your application process. Many ATS systems will allow you to automatically send out emails that walk applicants through your process. Send out automated messages that talk about phone screens, meeting with recruiters, preparing for interviews, or other updates.

2. Prepping Candidates

An important part of the recruiting process is just getting candidates prepared for the interview process. You can automate your prepping emails using (outlook template) by saving a template. I recommend showcasing interview tips like the STAR interview method or other YouTube video links that will help prepare for your candidate for the interview rounds.

3. Delivering updates

There is nothing worse than applying for a job and hearing nothing back, or only receiving minimal contact from the business. To make your candidates comfortable and to show that you value their time you should communicate regularly with them. Create specific communications at certain steps - an email to state you have received their application, and email to state their application was successful.

No matter the outcome, make sure to create a template that you send to candidates to give them the final update. This will help with your candidate experience goals. (Of course, follow up with a call when delivering the final round outcome).

4. Sending offers to accepted candidates

Make sure to send them a welcome to the team email and address general Q&A questions that they might have with onboarding.

5. Don't forget about referral leads generation

Once you've got a hired employee, make sure to follow up with them on how they are doing. Secondly, ask them for other leads or friends that they might have in their networks. Referral generation is a key part of sourcing.

Chapter 5: Creating Good Habits

Daily habits and structured routines will help you remain productive and create accountability for yourself. Creating these good habits starting on day one will make you successful no matter the outcome. Recruiting managers want to see your full output throughout the recruiting/sourcing funnel.

How many phone screens, business phones, and onsite final rounds are you averaging? This will paint a picture of what exactly you are accomplishing.

Every morning I write down what I want to accomplish for that day, whether it's the number of outreach messages or cold calls that I want to hit. When you track your sourcing KPI's you will start to see how many outreaches it takes to produce a hire.

For example, I know for a Software Engineer role: I want to average 15 phone screens per week and have 1-2 submittals for a business phone screen. From that, I want to get at least

8-9 onsite ready leads within that month. Thus averaging 1-2 hires for the start. Whatever role that you support, start by tracking your daily, weekly, and monthly KPI outputs. Then understand your average time to fill metrics.

Habits of successful recruiters

The best recruiters don't just perform based on intuition alone. Review some of the most effective habits to see what areas in your recruitment process could use fine-tuning for a more productive workflow.

1. Be proactive

Always be thinking about new ways to improve your recruiting process, whether it's through technology, collaboration, or simply asking yourself why something is happening the way it is—and if it could be done better.

2. Be consistent

Don't skip steps or take shortcuts just because they're easy or convenient at that moment. Consistency breeds trust, which breeds loyalty in candidates and clients who want to work with people they can count on (instead of being treated like just another number).

3. Be on time for anything and everything

This includes meetings with clients as well as internal deadlines for hiring managers and team members alike (and yes, even yourself). Don't let anyone down by showing up late—it won't go over well! People won't think highly of you if you show up later than expected without any notice ahead of time either; always give people plenty of notice when changing plans so everyone can adjust accordingly without having to scramble at the last minute.

3. Be accountable

Once you've established what needs to be done, the next step is making sure that it gets done. This is where self-accountability comes into play.

It's easy to let yourself slack off and do something else instead of doing the work that needs to be done. When this happens, it's important to have a system in place so that your productivity doesn't take a hit.

Try setting aside a regular time for checking in with yourself (you might try 30 minutes every morning). Having a method to track how you're doing will help keep you honest about whether you're following through with what's important—and if not, why bother?

Setting up daily goals

Whether you're an intern or an employee, setting goals is a great way to stay motivated and on-track. Still, goal setting can feel overwhelming—and the more ambitious the goal, the more daunting it feels to achieve it.

Fortunately, you don't have to take on everything at once. Daily goal setting is an incredibly manageable and rewarding strategy that can help you tackle those long-term objectives without the stress.

Here's a brief guide to get you started:

> 1. Make a list of what you want to accomplish each day—this helps keep you focused on what needs to get done, and it also serves as a record of what you've accomplished over time.
>
> 2. Break down those goals into smaller tasks—for example, if your goal is "create an email newsletter," then what are all the steps that go into making that happen?
>
> 3. Set mini deadlines for these tasks. For instance, you might want to send an email before lunch or schedule a meeting for the evening.

How to avoid distractions and streamline your workflow

When it comes to getting your work done and avoiding distractions, there are some simple steps you can take.

1. Choose a productive environment

First, if your office is noisy or messy, try to find a quiet place where you won't be distracted. Second, if your office is quiet but distracting for other reasons (like the fact that everyone around you is always talking about the latest news), then make sure that no one will bother you while working by putting on headphones or closing the door behind you.

2. Mute your Notifications

One thing that may become apparent when you start tracking your time is how often you check your emails throughout the day. While it might seem like a minute here and a minute there doesn't really matter, all those minutes start to add up. To make matters worse, some research suggests it can take up to 23 minutes to find your focus again after an interruption, making even the simplest task take a lot longer than it needs to.

To minimize your distractions, turn off notifications on all your devices — especially when you're tackling a task that requires your full attention. Dedicate specific windows to reading and responding to emails, like 15 minutes when you first get into the office and again after lunch, and try your best not to peek outside of those time frames. Closing the email tab on your computer altogether may help you resist the temptation.

If you're worried about missing something urgent, you can always add a little note to your email signature to set expectations and let people know how they can get your attention sooner if it's critical. That way, a candidate who thinks they're going to be late to their interview will now call you - if you don't immediately respond.

3. Don't be available all the time

It may be a difficult idea to get used to, but you don't need to answer every call, respond to every email, or attend every meeting you are invited to. Responding to every notification or ping instantly is a bad habit and you must work to break it. It takes a bit of training, but once your colleagues understand that you are not hyper-available, they'll leave you alone and only bother you with communications that are relevant.

4. Shorten your Recruiting Process

After pulling data or just seeing issues that arise in your process - make needed changes.

According to CareerBuilder, 60% of candidates stop filling out an online application that's too complicated. What's more, 54% of Gen Z job seekers won't even complete a job application if they suspect a company's recruiting methods are outdated.

If your application process is too long, overdue, or challenging, many job seekers will stop and switch to others. Thus, try to keep it as simple as possible. You can try out steps like eliminating cover letters, replacing long-term applications with a series of fast online queries, using mobile-friendly applications, and chatbots.

Chapter 6: Tracking your Time

Recruiters and Sourcers spend most of their time searching and responding to messages online. It's easy to have a ton of browser tabs open at a given time. You can easily get distracted by looking on social media or browsing online in general.

It's a good idea to track your overall time and what sites that you are visiting daily. It might make sense to block different sites like Facebook or Amazon if they become a major distraction.

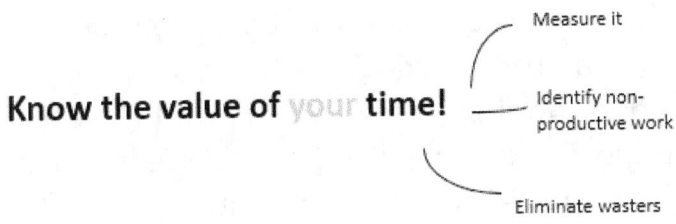

Tools to Track Your Time With

As familiar as your work schedule might be, it's often difficult to truly understand where you're spending most of your time during the day. Though it's easy to "guesstimate" how much attention you give different tasks, receiving accurate time tracking data can drastically help you streamline your efforts and boost productivity. Here are some tools worth considering.

1. Freedom

This simple app and website blocker have been trusted by millions of people to help them streamline their productivity. Users can schedule "Freedom time" in advance to block out portions of their day dedicated to distraction-free work circles, making it an invaluable resource for the modern recruiter.

2. TimeDoctor

TimeDoctor is a great option for an in-depth look into your productivity habits. The tool is primarily a time tracking solution that managers would use to oversee employees, but even solo workers can use it to receive insights into how they spend their time during the workday.

3. RescueTime

Another time management software, RescueTime is crafted to be a virtual productivity assistant that helps you redirect focus and avoid distractions. The tool can even tell you when the best times are for you to complete projects with maximum attention, help you avoid taking on too many tasks at once, and generate reports based on your performance.

4. Clockify
Able to integrate with over 50 web apps, Clockify is a straightforward Chrome expansion that offers a few time-saving features, such as idle detection, automatic reminders, work timers, and more. It can also track your time to help you see where your focus is most spent.

5. Simple Time Tracker
As the name suggests, this solution will keep tabs on where your efforts are being directed throughout the day. Recruiters can use these insights to identify whether they're spending too much time on e-mails, too little time on outreach, and more.

6. Toggl
This tool helps keep track of exactly how you're spending your time. The app lets you track individual tasks, or measure how long you're spending on different projects each week. It's essentially a timesheet, but it's a timesheet that gives you analytics at the end of every day to

show you exactly how you're spending your time and information to make the necessary changes.

7. Pomodoro - Tomato Timer

Do you find yourself hopping between tasks like a madman, juggling new emails with requests from your boss, jumping between candidate calls and email follow-ups? Again, you're not alone. Most of us, myself included, find it tough to settle down to a single task and get into what is known as our 'flow state.'

The Pomodoro Technique is a highly effective antidote for this. The tool will help create a cycle where you focus on your time in 30-minute sections.

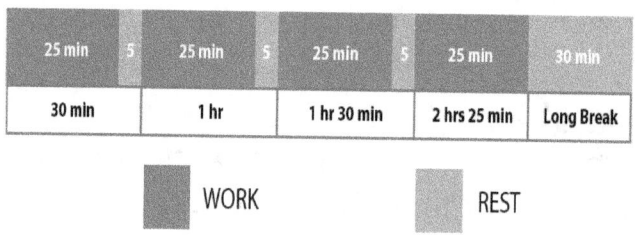

Use these time tracking tools to recognize your faults or other online distractors.

Avoiding Social Media

Like email, social media is an important tool for recruiters. But also, like email, it can kill as much productivity as it helps. Social media is one of the biggest drains on productivity in the US, as 60-80% report they go on social media for unnecessary tasks.

As a recruiter, the hardest part of using social media is knowing when you're doing something productive and when to quit because you're not getting anything done. Use tracking tools from the above suggestions to see how much certain social media sites are time wasters.

Recruiters can use social media tools like Hootsuite to automate different tasks, such as:

- Scheduling social media posts: Recruiters can use Hootsuite to schedule job postings, company updates, and other social media content in advance, saving time and ensuring that content is posted at optimal times.

- Monitoring social media mentions: Recruiters can use Hootsuite to monitor social media for mentions of their company or job openings and respond to inquiries or feedback in a timely manner.

- Tracking social media metrics: Recruiters can use Hootsuite to track social media metrics such as engagement, reach, and click-through rates, enabling them to measure the effectiveness of their social media campaigns.

- Automating social media campaigns: Recruiters can use Hootsuite to automate social media campaigns, such as promoting job openings, building brand awareness, or driving traffic to their career site.

- Collaborating with team members: Recruiters can use Hootsuite to collaborate with team members on social media campaigns, allowing them to assign tasks, provide feedback, and coordinate efforts more efficiently.

By using social media tools like Hootsuite, recruiters can automate different tasks and streamline their social media efforts, saving time and improving their social media presence.

Pulling RSS feeds to automatically post on social media channels:

To pull an RSS feed from a careers site to promote new job openings on social media automatically, you can follow these general steps:

- Check if the careers site has an RSS feed for job openings. Look for a link or icon that says "RSS" or "XML" on the site's careers page.

- Use an RSS feed reader tool to extract the RSS feed URL. Some examples of RSS feed reader tools are Feedly, Inoreader, and NewsBlur.

- Use a social media automation tool that supports RSS feeds. Some popular social media automation tools that support RSS feeds are Zapier, Hootsuite, and dlvr.it.

- Connect your RSS feed to your social media automation tool. Choose the social media platform where you want to post the job openings, and authorize the tool to access your account.

- Configure the settings for your automated posts. Choose how often you want the tool to check for new job openings on the RSS feed, and specify how you want the posts to appear on social media (e.g., with or without images, with specific hashtags).

- Test the automation to ensure that new job openings are being posted to social media automatically.

Chapter 7: Creating Goals and Tracking KPI Sourcing Metrics

If you're an HR professional, you know how important it is to have good sourcing metrics. You need to know the ROI of your hiring efforts and make sure they align with your overall business goals. The best way to do that is by tracking the right KPIs (key performance indicators). Here are four essential sourcing metrics that will help you track ROI, quality of hire, time-to-hire and candidate experience scores.

1. Time-to-hire

Time-to-hire is a common metric used to assess the effectiveness of your recruiting process. It's simply the average number of days it takes for you to fill a position.

2. Quality of hire

Quality of hire measures the quality of your candidates, their fit with the team, and their fit with the position.

The first step in measuring this is to set up an interview process that ensures you're only interviewing people who are qualified for your job openings. This may mean setting minimum qualifications (e.g., three years commercial experience or two years industry experience) to ensure they will be able to contribute effectively once hired.

3. Source of hire

Source of hire is a critical metric to track because it tells you where your best employees come from. If you're not hiring from the most effective sources, then it's likely that you will be spending more time on recruiting than necessary.

To start, ask yourself: "Where did I find my last 10 hires? And why were they good fits? Which sources are the most effective for finding new talent? Which ones don't work so well? Why do those differences exist? And how can I use this information to improve my sourcing strategy moving forward?"

4. Candidate experience score

Candidate experience is a key metric to track when it comes to sourcing strategy. A high-quality candidate experience speaks to the quality of your organization and can help you attract top talent.

You'll also want to benchmark yourself against other companies in similar industries by measuring how many applications come in per month or year (track this monthly), how many of those applications are rejected for no reason other than that they don't meet basic requirements (like having enough years of experience), and how many applicants make it through interviews before being declined or offered another role at another company.

Tracking KPIs and setting realistic expectations

If you're tracking KPIs, then you need to make sure that they are clearly defined. Define what success looks like and set appropriate benchmarks for each KPI so that everyone on your team knows what's expected of them.

Make sure everyone is clear on which metrics will be used to measure the success of their efforts and how those metrics can be tracked over time (monthly, quarterly or annually). Clay, Google Sheets, Excel, and Airtable are great options used by recruiters to track progress.

Still, remember to make your goals reasonable—both for yourself and the hiring managers you might work with. For instance, if you have a difficult manager who is demanding quick results, a fact-based analytics report can calm their expectations. Not everyone will fully understand what it takes to make a hire at your company, so having this information readily available can help bring them up to speed.

Create a dashboard in your ATS to automatically track your recruiting funnel metrics

- To create a dashboard in your ATS to automatically pull recruiting funnel metric data, you can follow these steps:

- Identify the key recruitment funnel metrics you want to track, such as the number of applicants, the number of interviews, and the number of hires.

- Choose an analytics tool that integrates with your ATS, such as Google Analytics or Microsoft Power BI.

- Connect your ATS to the analytics tool using the API or other integration methods provided by your ATS.

- Create a dashboard in the analytics tool to display the recruitment funnel metrics. Choose the data visualization type that best suits your needs, such as bar graphs, pie charts, or line charts.

- Set up automatic data pulls from your ATS to the analytics tool using the API or other integration methods. This will ensure that the data on the dashboard is always up-to-date.

- Customize the dashboard to display the recruitment funnel metrics in a way that is easy to understand and provides insights into your recruitment process. You can add filters, drill-down capabilities, and other interactive features to make the dashboard more user-friendly.

- Share the dashboard with relevant stakeholders, such as recruiters, hiring managers, and executives, to keep them informed about the recruitment process and enable data-driven decision making.

Chapter 8: Productivity Tools

The journey towards a perfectly productive workday is one that never truly ends. Still, there are thousands of solutions out there that can make it easier. These tools will help you remain productive and help automate mundane daily tasks, so you can finally focus on the recruitment part of your job. Here are some rapid-fire tech solutions that work great for any recruiter.

Email Resources

- **Checkmarks:** Simplify your email using Outlook's checkmark feature, which can signify which messages have been read. This tool helps you to stay organized using folders like a CRM tool.

- **Follow up scheduling:** Use this feature if you need to get in touch with a lead in the future. Use this to manage and automate notifications - so you don't forget to follow up with leads.

LinkedIn Tools

- **Use LinkedIn insights:** Need to quickly access market data? LinkedIn's Talent Insights platform can help you access crucial market data that covers everything from skill trends to current workforce benchmarks.

- **LinkedIn Recruiter Reports:** This feature can help you understand important data such as your email acceptance rates.

- **Send videos via LinkedIn messenger:** For conversations that would be best conducted in-person, try using the video feature on LinkedIn to enhance your communications with potential candidates without needing to schedule a meeting.

- **LinkedIn – pronunciation feature:** Use this tool to talk about jobs or employer branding efforts for your company instead of using it to pronounce your name

Notification Tools

- **Todoist:** This trusted task manager can help you track and organize your tasks, as well as send recurring reminders for upcoming deadlines.

- **Pushbullet:** You'll receive messages from almost every platform in existence as a recruiter. Pushbullet connects all your mobile devices and messaging apps, allowing you to manage your communications from a single place.

- **Google Voice:** This platform offers a feature that reads your emails out loud, allowing you to complete other tasks while still "reading" messages. You can then easily read through voicemail messages over your email.

Note Tracking Tools

- **OneNote:** As the name suggests, this fantastic app syncs directly with Outlook and your emails, keeping your workflow streamlined from start to finish.

- **Evernote:** Capable of syncing with LinkedIn profiles, this solution can be used for tracking and saving notes on individual leads (use this like a personal ATS).

- **Google Drive/Doc:** A classic resource across dozens of industries, these solutions let you save notes from any device at any location.

- **DropBox:** Another trusted and widely used option, you can use DropBox to store and track notes across multiple devices. I use this to manage my sourcing tracker / ATS documents it automatically saves and stores this valuable data all in one place.

Communication Tools

Teamwide communication:
- Trello
- Microsoft Teams
- Slack

Project management:
- Miro
- Monday
- Asana

How to track your emails

Email tracking tools are incredibly important for recruiters. You will need to track every email click and deliverability rate for each mail merge that you do.

So, which tool should you use? Well, there are quite a few great options on the market. Review the following to see which fits your needs best.

- **Streak for Gmail:** Streak sends you a notification every time your proposal is viewed—allowing you the perfect moment to send a follow up. It also doubles as a CRM tool!

- **SalesHandy:** This cold email outreach platform provides follow-up automation tools, email tracking, personalized replies, and so much more.

- **Bananatag:** This tool captures a diverse range of data you can use to propel your recruitment efforts, including email clicks, read time, device type, and more.

- **Yesware:** Another simplistic tool, Yesware notifies you whenever your emails are opened—as well as when the links within them are clicked on or viewed.

How to manage your emails

Tracking your emails is just one part of the recruitment process—keeping them managed is another story entirely. As you draft message after message, you might find your inbox cluttering up with responses. Fortunately, there are just as many tools designed to help keep the chaos organized.

- **Sortd**: This nifty tool lets you transform your static email inbox into a flexible set of lists and priorities. You can drag and drop emails between different lists, attach reminders or tasks to specific messages and generally make some sense of your inbox madness.

- **Boomerang:** This solution lets you take messages out of your inbox until you need them. Just click the Boomerang button when you open an email and choose when you need it again—it will archive your message for you. At the time you choose, it'll bring it back to your inbox, marked as unread, starred or even at the top of your message list. You can also use the plugin to schedule messages and set yourself reminders.

- **SaneBox:** Powered by AI, SaneBox can automatically sort your emails into separate folders. Mainly, it will place non-actionable emails aside, putting the most important messages onto your feed.

How to monitor your social media

Tracking your social media might sound like an unexpected part of a recruiter's job, yet it's one that only grows more important as the years pass. Platforms like LinkedIn and even TikTok have blossomed into major resources for recruiters—and you can use them to your advantage with a few neat tools.

- **Mentionlytics:** This platform is a marketer's dream come true, but it can also prove useful for general recruitment efforts. The tool will track and display crucial analytics such as "mention" insights, brand-related conversations, brand reputation trends, and more.

- **Page monitor:** This simple browser extension will send you notifications when a certain page has been updated online. Try using it to stay on top of a candidate's LinkedIn profile or a company's website!

- **Buffer:** Another all-in-one social media toolkit, Buffer offers a browser extension that reveals your brand's social media presence across every corner of the internet. You can use it to access comments, plan campaigns, and more.

- **Hootsuite:** This dashboard offers extensive social listening capabilities, revealing current trends and content insights that can help you nail down the best candidates.

- **Google Alerts:** Like page monitor, Google Alerts follows the same concept by tracking specific topics with a broader focus. Try using it to track a Boolean string and use the advanced filters to narrow down results based on webs source and location.

How to track your sourcing KPI metrics

It's very important to track every lead that you've contacted and submitted to your job requisitions. Doing so will give you a clear picture of your pipeline and what it takes to source, recruit, and hire a candidate. The metrics you'll want to collect include:

- % of response rates you receive
- % of people you contact who are QIA
- % of candidates who pass the prescreens
- % of candidates you select for interview
- % of candidates you send an offer to
- % of candidates who accept your final-offer

Once you've reached out and acquired this information, you'll need a way to store this data so you can use it to measure your successes. Fortunately, there are more than a few simple solutions at any recruiter's disposal.

- **Onenote:** An add-in you can activate within Outlook, this tool syncs your documents and other notes into one portal for convenient access.

- **Google Sheets:** A free solution bundled with Google Drive; you'll easily find dozens of pre-made Google Sheets templates for recruitment tracking on the internet. Just copy and paste them into your own to immediately start tracking your metrics.

- **Excel:** A long trusted spreadsheet tool, Excel is a great — albeit complicated — way to start tracking your sourcing KPI metrics. There are numerous tips and tricks you should familiarize yourself with to get the most out of the resource and limit frustration. Some of these include:

    o Select all cells by clicking the gray triangle in your spreadsheet's top left corner
    o Format numbers by selecting a column and pressing Ctrl – Shift - $
    o Jump to the top of your spreadsheet by pressing Command + Up Arrow Twice

Excel Shortcuts:

Recruiters can use several Excel shortcuts to work more efficiently and save time. Here are some useful Excel shortcuts for recruiters:

Ctrl + C and Ctrl + V: Copy and paste data quickly.

Ctrl + X: Cut data.

Ctrl + Z: Undo the last action.

Ctrl + Y: Redo the last action.

Ctrl + F: Find data in the spreadsheet.

Ctrl + H: Replace data in the spreadsheet.

Ctrl + A: Select all data in the spreadsheet.

Ctrl + B: Bold selected text or cells.

Ctrl + I: Italicize selected text or cells.

Ctrl + U: Underline selected text or cells.

Ctrl + 1: Open the Format Cells dialog box.

Ctrl + Shift + L: Turn on/off filters.

Alt + Down Arrow: Display the drop-down menu for a selected cell.

F2: Edit the active cell.

F4: Repeat the last action.

F7: Spell check selected text or cells.

F11: Create a chart based on selected data.

Shift + F3: Open the Insert Function dialog box.

Shift + F11: Insert a new worksheet.

Shift + Arrow Keys: Select a range of cells.

By using these shortcuts, recruiters can work more efficiently in Excel and save time.

Excel Formulas:

Recruiters can use several Excel formulas to help manage their data and analyze candidate information. Here are some useful Excel formulas for recruiters:

COUNTIF: Count the number of cells in a range that meet a certain criteria. For example, =COUNTIF(A2:A10, "Sales") would count the number of cells in range A2:A10 that contain the word "Sales".

SUMIF: Add up the values in a range that meet a certain criteria. For example, =SUMIF(A2:A10, "Sales", B2:B10) would add up the values in column B that correspond to the cells in column A that contain the word "Sales".

VLOOKUP: Look up a value in a table and return a corresponding value from a specified column. For example, =VLOOKUP("John", A2:B10, 2, FALSE) would search for the name "John" in column A and return the corresponding value in column B.

CONCATENATE: Combine two or more text strings into one. For example, =CONCATENATE(A2, " ", B2) would combine the text in cells A2 and B2 with a space in between.

IF: Perform a logical test and return one value if the test is true and another value if the test is false. For example, =IF(C2>=75, "Pass", "Fail") would return the word "Pass" if the value in cell C2 is greater than or equal to 75 and "Fail" if it is less than 75.

LEFT/RIGHT/MID: Extract a specified number of characters from the beginning (LEFT), end (RIGHT), or middle (MID) of a text string. For example, =LEFT(A2, 3) would return the first three characters of the text in cell A2.

AVERAGE: Calculate the average of a range of values. For example, =AVERAGE(B2:B10) would calculate the average of the values in column B from row 2 to row 10.

AX/MIN: Find the maximum or minimum value in a range of values. For example, =MAX(C2:C10) would find the highest value in column C from row 2 to row 10.

By using these formulas, recruiters can manage and analyze their data more effectively in Excel.

More Tool Options:

Browser Extensions

- **WhenX:** This candidate tracking tool helps recruiters add candidates to their pipeline for later action. For instance, you can save a candidate's LinkedIn profile and status along with a note, which is automatically applied to your search results. If you later search for a role, your note will be displayed alongside their search result.

- **Onetab:** If you use Google Chrome, OneTab allows you to store your open tabs into one neat list. This doesn't only save your computer's memory, but it also allows you to easily retrieve a previous candidate's profile by searching through one neat list — rather than navigate thousands of search results again.

Editing

- **Grammarly:** This grammar and spellchecker is a great extension for keeping your e-mails professional and error-free.

- **Wordtune:** Powered by AI, this is a writing companion that can suggest different sentence structures and edit your written work.

- **Microsoft Editor:** Microsoft's free spelling and grammar checker is a no-brainer — add it to your document for instant polish.

- **MultiHighlighter:** This Chrome extension will highlight your desired keywords on any webpage in just a few clicks.

Task Management

- **MeisterTask:** This software features built-in time tracking tools and a task dashboard that helps users divert their focus more effectively.

- **BIGContacts:** A CRM software, BIGContacts is a great way to simplify your workflow by keeping your tasks in one platform, automating repetitive actions, and setting reminders for upcoming deadlines.

- **Tasklog:** Though primarily designed for freelancers, Tasklog is a great option for anyone who largely does independent work. Its to-do-list and project management functions can help you visual you're pacing throughout the workday.

Chapter 9: Automation Tools

Automation tools are a great way to save time on the entire hiring process. As you already know, much of recruitment relies on repetitive tasks that can quickly become monotonous. Still, *someone* will need to oversee them for your efforts to be successful—luckily, technology can do the job.

Using automation tools can help recruiters work more efficiently, improve the candidate experience, and make data-driven decisions, ultimately leading to better recruitment outcomes.

1. **Saves time:** Automation tools can automate repetitive and time-consuming tasks, such as sending follow-up emails, scheduling interviews, and posting job listings on social media, allowing recruiters to focus on more strategic and high-value tasks.

2. **Increases efficiency:** Automation tools can streamline the recruitment process and reduce errors, improving efficiency and enabling recruiters to manage more candidates at once.

3. **Improves candidate experience:** Automation tools can help recruiters provide a better candidate experience by sending timely and personalized communications, providing immediate feedback, and reducing wait times.

4. **Provides data insights:** Automation tools can track and analyze recruitment data, providing insights into the recruitment process and enabling recruiters to make data-driven decisions.

5. **Enhances collaboration:** Automation tools can facilitate collaboration among recruiters and other stakeholders, allowing them to share information and work together more effectively.

1. Zapier

Zapier is great for automating repetitive tasks (even between different apps) as well as making processes easier and faster for employees or users who perform them on a regular basis. For example, if you have several new hires who are starting their first day at your company and need to be added to payroll and other systems, Zapier can be used to automate the process of adding that person's information into the system.

2. Airtable

Airtable is an app that is like a spreadsheet, but it also has a CRM feature. This makes it great for organizing candidates and hiring managers, and for gathering interviewers.

To use Airtable, you'll need to create a new table within the app. For example, you could have a table called "Candidates" with columns like name, email address and phone number. Then add rows for each candidate in the database by clicking on the plus sign at the bottom left of your screen.

If you want this to be private information only accessible by yourself or other admins within your company (and not available publicly), then click on "Advanced" before entering names into these fields so that they are hidden from everyone else who uses Airtable—but still accessible by any admins within your organization.

3. IFTTT

IFTTT (If This, Then That) is a free tool that lets you create recipes to automate tasks. For example, if you want to send an email introducing yourself to every new LinkedIn contact, you can set up a recipe that sends the email when they connect with you. Or maybe you'd prefer to add their contact information directly in your Google Drive spreadsheet? You can do that too!

IFTTT has over 700 different apps and services it works with, so there's no limit on what kind of automation recipes you might come up with.

3. PhantomBuster

This cloud-based software is especially useful for recruiters, as it relies on data extraction to automate users' desired processes. Some of its potential uses include automatically accepting LinkedIn invitations, sending personalized LinkedIn messages on your behalf, and finding Instagram/Facebook URLS based on full names and company names.

4. HubSpot

A CRM tool trusted by thousands of businesses, HubSpot's capabilities make it a versatile solution that can also be utilized by recruiters. Its automation functionality can power a range of sourcing efforts: for instance, HubSpot can automatically send emails to candidates if a hiring manager is interested in scheduling a phone interview.

5. BlockSpring

BlockSpring is a tool that allows you to automate your marketing reports. The tool can work with Google Sheets, Excel, and Tableau, saving you from needing to manually refresh reports each time.

6. SeekOut

Automated sourcing tools leverage AI to identify passive candidates who hold the skills and experience that align with the roles you're hiring for, saving recruiters countless hours scrolling through profiles on LinkedIn.

Of these, SeekOut is one of the best options: an all-in-one tool helps recruiters find and engage external candidates. Users can upload a job description, which the tool will use to automatically find and source leads. They can then select good fits from this list and automatically schedule email sequence campaigns.

7. Magical

Magical is the fastest way to source candidates, update your ATS, and send pre-populated template messages that convert. It's an all-in-one automation tool that sync's different tools together like Zapier.

One-click automation

Populate sourcing sheets, candidate responses, or your ATS database, without the exhausting copy-and-paste between tabs.

Works where you do

Supercharge your productivity in places you already work, like LinkedIn, Gmail, Workday, or even your internal HR and recruiting sites.

Set up in seconds
Magical doesn't rely on integrations, APIs, or complex workflow builders. Just download and start automating your workflow now.

5. Chat GPT – AI Writing Tool

For years now there has been a prediction about how AI is going to take over recruiting. So far there have been some tools that have helped recruiters be more efficient and better, but most of the tools out there so far have not lived up to the hype.

In comes, Open AI's Chat GPT-3 which I know is not going to replace any recruiters at the moment, but it's the best AI tool that has been released to the public.

How can you use this tool with messaging?
Use AI to reach out to potential candidates through personalized emails or messages,

inviting them to apply for a job or to learn more about the organization.

Once you create an account you can ask this AI tool virtually any type of question. So, I decided to ask it how to write effective recruiter messages and here's the result.

[Write a Short Example of Outreach to a Potential Candidate About a Data Science Job...]

Hi [Candidate],
I hope this message finds you well. My name is [Your Name] and I am a recruiter with [Company Name]. I came across your LinkedIn profile and was impressed by your background in data science.

I wanted to reach out to see if you might be interested in a data science opportunity that we have available at our company. The role involves working on a range of data-driven projects, using a variety of tools and techniques to analyze and interpret data.

We are looking for someone with strong problem-solving skills and a passion for data.

I would love to speak with you more about this opportunity and see if it might be a good fit for you.

If you are interested, please don't hesitate to reach out to me to schedule a call at your convenience.

Best regards,
[Your Name]

Other Automation Tools

Phone Call & Text Message Automation

- **Honeit Software:** This all-in-one platform is a perfect companion to your interviewing process, as it can automatically record and generate insights for each conversation in real-time.

- **Google Voice:** From automatic forwarding to accurate call tracking, Google Voice is a simple tool that any recruiter will find useful — it's even accessible from both mobile and desktop devices.

- **iPhone:** iOS 13 introduced "Shortcuts", which is iPhones way of automating repeated tasks. Recruiters can use this to instantly begin screen recording interview phone calls (with consent, of course) without having to interrupt the conversation.

- **SimpleTexting Tool:** This leading tool grants users access to SMS campaign creation, organized contact lists, and more.

Chatbot Automation

- **Paradox:** Designed specifically for recruiters, Paradox's AI assistant, Olivia, can help you screen candidates, reply to inquiries, and much more to secure leads from your career site.

- **Facebook Messenger Bots:** Add any chatbot to your Facebook page to create automatic greetings, program answers, and even complete tasks on your behalf.

LinkedIn Message Automation:

- **Textexpander:** Auto-fill in pre-vetted templates for emails or other messages in just a few clicks! This is a HUGE time saver tool and only costs a few dollars per month to have access to.

- **Very Fast Extension:** Create lightning-fast auto-responses using this straightforward shortcut tool.

- **WebbTree:** Discover and engage candidates with automated feedback collection and other sourcing solutions.

- **SourceWhale:** Automate your daily recruiting tasks using various integrations and detailed insights.

- **Jobin.cloud:** Streamline your outreach methods, track messages, and more with diverse automation functionalities.

AI Searching Automation

- **SeekOut:** This all-in-one tool helps recruiters find and engage external candidates. Users can upload a job description, which the tool will use to automatically find and source leads. They can then select good fits from this list and automatically schedule email sequence campaigns.

Email Merging and Email Campaign Software Tools

- **Saleshandy:** It's worth re-mentioning this favorite mail merging tool thanks to its exceptional cold email outreach functionalities.

- **MailShake:** Connect to your email platform, CRM, and other tools for streamlined access to recruitment communications.

- **Lemlist:** Personalize your cold emails, engage with a larger number of leads, and automate your follow-up messages with this comprehensive solution.

- **Gem:** Utilize the power of data to improve your candidate experience and establish robust talent pipelines. Create email sequencing campaigns with ease and easily import the leads into your ATS or CRM systems.

- **Word/Excel:** Recruiters can also use mail merge on either of these tools using their built-in features.

Calendar Scheduling and Management Tools

- **Calendly:** Streamline your focus by allowing this simple tool to schedule meetings on your behalf.

- **Prelude:** Designed specifically for interviews, Prelude is a great way to improve candidate experience for both phone screenings and onsite evaluations.

- **Acuity:** This solution allows candidates to choose a date amongst your existing schedule, which is then synced to your current calendar (Google, Outlook, or iCal).

Automating Tasks or Sequences in your ATS system

To automate different tasks in your ATS system, you can follow these general steps:

- Identify the tasks that you want to automate, such as sending follow-up emails, scheduling interviews, or updating candidate statuses.

- Choose an automation tool that integrates with your ATS system. Some popular automation tools that integrate with ATS systems include Zapier, Workato, and Tray.io.

- Connect your ATS system to the automation tool using the API or other integration methods provided by your ATS system.

- Choose the automation workflow you want to create based on the tasks you want to automate. For example, if you want to send a follow-up email to candidates after they apply, you can create a workflow that triggers an email to be sent when a candidate submits an application.

- Configure the automation workflow by setting up triggers, conditions, and actions. Triggers are events that start the workflow, conditions are criteria that determine when the workflow is executed, and actions are the tasks that are performed by the workflow.

- Test the automation workflow to ensure that it works as expected. Test the workflow with a small sample of data to avoid any unintended consequences.

- Monitor the automation workflow and make adjustments as needed. Continuously monitor the automation workflow to ensure that it is performing as expected and make adjustments as needed to improve performance.

Chapter 10: Working with Hiring Managers

Setting clear expectations and holding hiring managers accountable will help alleviate problems down the road. Having an engaged hiring team will make you way more productive and fill the roles.

Setting up Realistic Expectations with your Hiring Managers

First, you'll need to help your hiring manager understand what to expect during your relationship. You can do this by following these steps:

- **Step One:** Schedule intake calls to understand their needs.

- **Step Two:** Discuss and establish a realistic timeline between sourcing candidates and filling the position.

- **Step Three:** Discuss their communication commitment (i.e., how timely they'll respond to your follow-up questions, etc.).

As amiable as your relationship might be, your hiring manager will still regularly want to see results. That's why it's important to always have an updated sourcing tracker document that showcases your weekly and monthly recruiting KPI metrics.

I also recommend pulling internal data from your ATS or CRM to showcase this data during your intake or bi-weekly update meetings with hiring managers. You will need to set clear expectations with your hiring managers to be successful long term.

Turn your Hiring Managers into Sourcers

Now, let's say your hiring manager is creating urgency on a particular req. The market is incredibly tough but your hiring manager might not know that. So, another way to humble a hiring manager is to have them directly source with you. Create a project and have them do the outreach attempts. This will help them understand the level of difficulty recruiters are facing in this current market.

A majority of roles usually get filled by my team referrals. It is important to build relationships with your hiring managers and their teams.

Sourcing is a highly time-consuming part of a recruiter's role. Instead of working longer, why not work smarter?

Note: Share a google sheets sourcing tracker document with your hiring team. Use this showcase weekly metrics and goals.

Use your Hiring teams for referral drive automation

Productive recruiters know they can't do it all on their own. They need to work closely with hiring managers and the interview team to make sure everyone is aligned.

There are many benefits to employee referrals such as reduced costs per hire, improved quality of hire, reduced turnover, increased profits and producing the best return on investment. Recruiters should actively communicate referral incentives to their teams to turn high-quality candidates into long-lasting employees.

Referral Strategies:

- **Create a Sourcing Jam Event:** As you can guess, this involves setting up a teamwide event dedicated to talent sourcing. Here, you'll work together by going through each member's network for potential leads, as well as generating outreach methods for passive leads.

- **Gamify Your Referrals:** "Gamifying" your employee referral program can also be incredibly effective. Some popular methods include offering incentives to those who's referrals lead to the most hires, granting "points" for each referral (which can be applied towards prizes), and more!

Depending on the size of your Talent Acquisition, it always makes sense to internally network. I've made a ton of connections just by sharing my network with other fellow recruiters or leaders in my niche.

Standardize Your Interview Structure

Your interview process should be the same for every qualified candidate. To ensure this is the case, we recommend that you standardize your interview structure. This can be done by following these steps.

- Develop a list of must-haves for any role you are hiring for.

- Create interview questions that focus on the skills and experience that are most important for the role
- Ask the same questions of every candidate to make a fair comparison

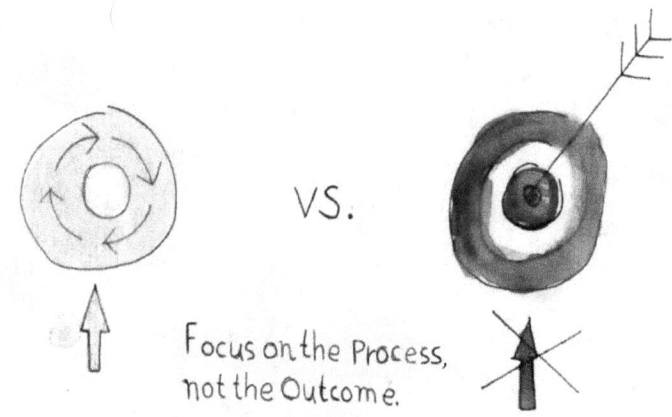

Focus on the Process, not the Outcome.

Automate follow ups with hiring managers

- To automate follow-ups with hiring managers for recruiting updates on roles, you can follow these general steps:

- Choose an automation tool that integrates with your ATS system and email client, such as Zapier, Workato, or IFTTT.

- Create a new automation workflow that triggers an email to the hiring manager when a certain event occurs, such as a candidate moving to the next stage in the recruitment process.

- Configure the workflow to send a follow-up email to the hiring manager if they do not respond to the initial email within a specified timeframe.

- Personalize the follow-up email by including the name of the hiring manager and the details of the role they are hiring for.

- Schedule the follow-up emails to be sent automatically based on the timeframe you have set. This can be done using the scheduling features of your automation tool.

- Test the automation workflow with a small sample of data to ensure that it is working as expected.

- Monitor the workflow to ensure that it is sending the follow-up emails on schedule and adjust the timing or content of the emails as needed.

By following these steps, you can automate follow-ups with hiring managers for recruiting updates on roles, reducing the need for manual follow-up emails and improving the efficiency of your recruitment process.

Summary

In this book, you've learned some of the most powerful tips to become a more productive and organized recruiter throughout your day.

As a recruiter, time management is essential to your success. Here are some tips to help you manage your time effectively:

Create a daily schedule: Start by creating a schedule for your day. This should include all the tasks you need to complete, including sourcing candidates, screening resumes, conducting interviews, and following up with clients. Set specific times for each task and stick to your schedule as closely as possible.

Prioritize your tasks: Once you have your schedule, prioritize your tasks. Focus on the most important tasks first, such as filling urgent positions or following up with key clients. This will help you stay on track and ensure that you are making progress towards your goals.

Use automation tools: There are many automation tools available to recruiters, such as applicant tracking systems and email templates. These tools can help you save time by streamlining your workflow and automating repetitive tasks.

Streamline your communication: Communication is a critical part of recruiting, but it can also be a major time sink. To streamline your communication, consider using email templates, scheduling tools, and other communication tools to reduce the time you spend on administrative tasks.

Focus on quality over quantity: While it can be tempting to try to fill as many positions as possible, focusing on quality over quantity can actually save you time in the long run. By focusing on finding the best candidates for each position, you can reduce the amount of time you spend on screening and interviewing candidates who are not a good fit.

Take breaks: Finally, don't forget to take breaks throughout the day. Taking short breaks can help you recharge and stay focused, which will ultimately make you more productive in the long run.

Let's review what we went over in each chapter:

Chapter 1: Learning how to set yourself up for long term success

Chapter 2: Staying organized

Chapter 3: Time management best practices

Hacks

- Time Tracking Tools
- Time Management
- Calendar Time Blocking
- Setting Daily Goals

Chapter 4: How to manage your calendar schedule well

Chapter 5: Creating good habits

- Unlearn bad habits
- Creating a positive mindset
- Building a life outside of work

Chapter 6: Tracking your time and learning how to avoid other distractions.

Hacks

- Creating a Sourcing KPI Tracker
- Tracking Emails and Calls

Chapter 7: Productivity tools to help organize and focus on your efforts

Hacks:

- Email Tracking / Clicks
- Email Mail merge
- Calendar Scheduling Tools

Chapter 8: Time saving productivity tools

Chapter 9: Automation tools that integrate and sync with each other

Chapter 10: Building relationships with hiring managers and interviewing teams

Conclusion

I hope you've gained insights on time management and have found value from these chapters.

I've written on several topics within recruiting and have received so many kind notes and messages from recruiters across the world. I can't thank you enough for that. It has enlightened and humbled me greatly.

I would appreciate it if you would take the time to write an honest review about the book on Amazon so that others can also benefit from this publication.

Appendix

Page 13: Streetsweb.co.uk
Page 19: Metaphoricmath.com
Page 21: Lifehack.org
Page 32: LinkedIn.com
Page 36: Gmail.com
Page 37: Outlook.com

www.ingramcontent.com/pod-product-compliance
Lightning Source LLC
Chambersburg PA
CBHW070241220526
45465CB00004B/1482